God's Kind of Faith

By Aaron Winter

Revival Waves of Glory
Books & Publishing

Litchfield, IL 62056
http://www.revivalwavesofgloryministries.com

God's Kind of Faith

COVER ARTWORK CREATED BY: DANIELA OWERGOOR

CONTACT DANIELA OWERGOOR AT: P.X.DANY@GMAIL.COM

EBook: 978-1-312-02724-4

Paperback: 978-1-312-02721-3

Hardcover: 978-1-312-02722-0

TABLE OF CONTENTS

Dedication

This book is dedicated first and foremost to God the Father who is our great I AM & is the Ancient of Days who sits on the throne of heaven; to Jesus Christ of Nazareth for ransoming me through the merciful work on the cross, so that I could become a son that stands, serves, ministers, and burn as a holy priest in His Kingdom. Thank You Holy Spirit of God who is the source of all wisdom and revelation.

A close second, is to my beautiful and amazing wife, Shannon, my best friend, whose support throughout the writing of this book was immeasurable. Her purity of heart and faith are always a source of inspiration and strength.

About the Author

Aaron Winter is the President of Hearts of Fire International Ministries & is the television host of Hearts of Fire TV. Operating with a powerful anointing with a prophetic edge, his message of walking in God's power and understanding our true identity in Christ has changed lives all over the world through conferences, seminars, and in evangelistic crusades that include audiences that have exceeded 100,000 people. Aaron has authored: Becoming a Heart of Fire, Bible Prayers, God's Kind of Faith and soon to be released Heavenly Realities.

Aaron received his Doctorate in Divinity from Destiny Christian University in 2014 and graduated from Portland Bible College, earning his bachelor degree in Theology in 2003.

Endorsements

God's Kind of Faith will captivate your mind and engage your spirit. Dr. Aaron Winter explains faith in a way that is both profound and easy to understand. Today, I encourage you to read this book and do what it says, so you can win the world around you for Christ.

Kumar Raju Komannapalli
President, Jesus for All Generations Ministries

I have known Aaron Winter for several years and in this current age of low commitment I've found Aaron to be the exception in his generation.

His depth of commitment to the Lord and to Spirit filled ministry is evident in all areas of his life. While I pastored New Life in Sherwood, Aaron was a faithful member and we've worked together on several projects.

I highly recommend Aaron, this book and Hearts of Fire International Ministries.

Pastor Jeff Dorothy
Faith Center, Salem Oregon

Introduction

In 2011, God told me to do a series on Faith. This gave me a great deal of excitement, and expectation that God was going to do something miraculous. As I began to pray into it, the Lord revealed to me that the Body of Christ as a whole had lost faith, thus God led me to do a series on faith because it plays such a key role in the life of believers.

When I began, I started to understand why the Church had lost it's of understanding faith. Out of all the books, videos and other materials that could be found on the subject, they were vague, incomplete, or misleading.

Part of the problem was that even the leadership of the Body of Christ didn't have a clear understanding of what faith is, nor did the Church have a working knowledge of how to use it. Faith comes by hearing and hearing by a word of God, and if the Body of Christ doesn't hear about faith, then they won't have much of it to work with.

Thus, I began the series by first defining what faith is and then expounding on it from there, attempting to cover every angle. Within this book, I will give in detail the discoveries that I have made during that series and give you workable knowledge that you can apply in your life.

Chapter One

What is Faith?

The intent of this book is to develop a theological platform that will enhance the Body of Christ's awareness of faith by first coming to a better understanding of what faith is, how it operates and then how it can be applied in our everyday lives.

To fully understand faith, we must realize that the invisible supernatural dimensions of heaven are as real as the one we can see with our own eyes. Just because we cannot see it, doesn't mean it does not exist. For instance, we cannot see oxygen; however it is vital to every living human being for our continued existence. It would be erroneous to imply that oxygen is fiction just because it is not seen in the natural by our own two eyes.

2 Corinthians 4:18 says:

> WHILE WE LOOK NOT AT THE THINGS WHICH ARE SEEN, BUT AT THE THINGS WHICH ARE NOT SEEN; FOR THE THINGS WHICH ARE SEEN ARE TEMPORAL; BUT THE THINGS WHICH ARE NOT SEEN ARE ETERNAL.

Developing faith that is alive and active is vital to the walk of every believer. Faith by its very nature is alive, it is active, and connects believers through the Holy Spirit to Jesus Christ. Faith is a key that unlocks things in the heavens and brings them into the earth. It creates an open door by which the reality of Christ becomes manifest on the Earth.

In fact, God has given us a set of keys to establish His kingdom, and faith is one of those keys. Jesus said in Matthew 16:19: "I WILL GIVE YOU THE KEYS OF THE KINGDOM; AND WHATEVER YOU BIND ON EARTH WILL BE BOUND IN HEAVEN, AND WHATEVER YOU LOOSE ON EARTH WILL BE LOOSED IN HEAVEN."

By exercising the key of faith, we can use it to bind up demons and loosen the saving, healing, and delivering power of God in the earth just as it is in heaven.

Jesus said in Matthew 13:31-32: "THE KINGDOM OF HEAVEN IS LIKE A MUSTARD SEED, WHICH A MAN TOOK AND PLANTED IN HIS FIELD. THOUGH IT IS THE SMALLEST OF ALL SEEDS, YET WHEN IT GROWS, IT IS THE LARGEST OF GARDEN PLANTS AND BECOMES A TREE SO BIG THAT BIRDS OF THE AIR COME AND PERCH IN ITS BRANCHES...."

Later in chapter 17, a man approaches Jesus, kneels before him, and says: "LORD, HAVE MERCY ON MY SON, HE HAS SEIZURES AND IS SUFFERING GREATLY. HE OFTEN FALLS INTO THE FIRE OR INTO THE LAKE. I BROUGHT HIM TO YOUR DISCIPLES, BUT THEY COULD NOT HEAL HIM." Jesus then rebukes the demon within the child and the child was healed instantly.

Later on his disciples are embarrassed and asked why they could not drive out the demon.

Jesus says this:

"BECAUSE YOU HAVE SO LITTLE FAITH. I TELL YOU THE TRUTH, IF YOU HAVE FAITH AS SMALL AS A MUSTARD SEED, YOU CAN SAY TO THIS MOUNTAIN, 'MOVE FROM HERE TO THERE' AND IT WILL MOVE. NOTHING WILL BE IMPOSSIBLE FOR YOU."

Jesus' response to His disciples was full of insight into the topic of faith for that generation. Now I don't know about you, but I did not grow up on a farm, so maybe you're like me, and have actually never seen a mustard seed in person.

Jesus spoke of the mustard seed because the culture was an agricultural society that needed crops and gardens for economic livelihood. Therefore, Jesus was actually speaking their common everyday language. He was communicating to them about both the Kingdom of God and faith using common everyday items to which they were familiar with.

In today's technological world, we could compare faith to items that we use today that have the same kind of effect. A microchip perhaps works as a great example of an extremely small component that can perform at very high levels.

For instance, Jesus today could say of faith: "IF YOU HAVE FAITH AS SMALL AS A MICROCHIP YOU CAN MOVE THE ENTIRE WORLD FROM ONE PLACE TO ANOTHER. AND NOTHING WOULD BE IMPOSSIBLE FOR YOU."

Therefore, just like the mustard seed, the value of a microchip is not in its individual size. Other every day household items could even work as a great example. An electric fuse is small yet carries enough power to light up an entire building or even an entire city of buildings.

The conductive nature of these everyday products is the key. Microchips transfer data to wherever they are directed. Electric fuses transfer power from its original source to wherever it is directed. In other words, today's technological tools have the capabilities of transferring large amounts of data and power which can in the right setting and in the right hands, literally move the entire world from one place to another. Faith is similar. Faith transfers the power from God (the source) to wherever it is needed.

Maybe in your home or workplace there is a Wi-Fi connection to link your computer or phone to the internet; well faith is the link that connects you to God.

For a moment, let us think about an electric fuse. A fuse from the inside is made up of metal, such as silver wire, which is conductive to electricity as it offers low resistance to electronic currents. Thus it is able to carry electric power from one place to another.

Now if we were to examine the metal *lead* for instance, instead of silver, we would get a different outcome. Lead is highly resistant to electricity, and is incapable of carrying any kind of electric current.

In the Spirit, this looks like this:

When we are receptive to the leading of the Holy Spirit, we become conductive to His current, and are able to access heaven into the Earth. On the flip side of that, fuses with high resistance will either not carry any power or it will get overwhelmed and blow up. If we resist the Holy Spirit with unbelief, then we are not conductive to Him, and the power of God will not manifest.

Jesus was amazed in many of the places he ministered in because of their unbelief; and it was because of this (their unbelief), that Jesus was only able to do a handful of miracles in certain locations. In other words, even Jesus Christ Himself was handicapped by the **unbelief** of entire towns.

If we are full of unbelief which is similar to the metal lead, with high resistance to the things of the Holy Spirit, then we will not be conductive to the current of electronic power of Heaven… It will just remain there and not invade earth.

The world has some crazy notions about what faith healers are all about. They think that the faith healers manifest some power in and of themselves. Look, people do not have any kind of real power. People are not generators of power, but conductors of power. We are vessels, the channels that God's power flows through, not the source itself.

Jesus said in John 15:4: "AS THE BRANCH CANNOT BEAR FRUIT OF ITSELF, UNLESS IT ABIDES IN THE VINE, NEITHER CAN YOU, UNLESS YOU ABIDE IN ME."

Reinhard Bonnke said this:

"Faith is like a wiring system that carries power into our lives. The wiring system carries power but does not create power. Faith in of itself only carries power, but faith is not power, it only links us to the power source. However this is vital: there is no link to God without faith." [1]

If I could define faith in simple terms, I would say "Faith is being plugged into God; it is the plugging in that is faith."

The Biblical definition of faith is found in Hebrews 11:1: "NOW FAITH IS THE SUBSTANCE OF THINGS HOPED FOR, THE EVIDENCE OF THINGS NOT SEEN."

Throughout history, people wondered what does this mean, faith is substance? Is it tangible? Indeed, faith is a substance that serves as a title/deed laid up in heaven regarding the promises of God that are hoped for by our Spirit, it is *the* evidence, *the* proof of those things

---

[1] Faith – The Link with God's Power by Reinhard Bonnke

that through Christ are ours, by which we claim by conviction by the Spirit.

Faith is able to grab hold of what the Spirit discerns as real fact, even before it has been revealed to the natural senses. It is in *this* realm where miracles can happen. To grasp this concept we must realize that the spiritual dimensions are more real than the natural.

2 Corinthians 4:18 says:

WHILE WE LOOK NOT AT THE THINGS WHICH ARE SEEN, BUT AT THE THINGS WHICH ARE NOT SEEN: FOR THE THINGS WHICH ARE SEEN ARE TEMPORAL; BUT THE THINGS WHICH ARE NOT SEEN ARE ETERNAL.

Everything in the natural was made up by the spiritual, namely from the supernatural God in heaven.

Colossians 1:16 says:

"FOR BY HIM ALL THINGS WERE CREATED: THINGS IN HEAVEN AND ON EARTH, VISIBLE AND INVISIBLE, WHETHER THRONES OR POWERS OR RULERS OR AUTHORITIES; ALL THINGS WERE CREATED BY HIM AND FOR HIM. HE IS BEFORE ALL THINGS, AND IN HIM ALL THINGS HOLD TOGETHER."

Friends, our God created the heavens and the Earth, the invisible and the visible and they are all held under His command. In addition, God blesses us with access to His greatness in every way.

Ephesians 1:3 says:

"PRAISE BE TO GOD AND FATHER OF OUR LORD JESUS CHRIST, WHO HAS BLESSED US IN THE HEAVENLY REALMS WITH EVERY SPIRITUAL BLESSING."

Even though we are still on this temporal planet, in the spirit we are seated positionally with Christ.

Ephesians 2:6 says:

"AND GOD RAISED US UP WITH CHRIST AND SEATED US WITH HIM IN THE HEAVENLY REALMS IN CHRIST JESUS."

Ladies and gentleman, we have access to these spiritual blessings because Christ has positionally seated us with Him at the right hand of God. This means when we align ourselves in that position, we are coming into "Faith" and by coming into faith we are able to take hold of the spiritual promises and blessings which are ours because we are now heirs with Christ.

Faith doesn't just believe with nothing special in mind. It believes unto something for something. The Word of God gives point, direction, and purpose. Need a new leg, a new knee, how about a new liver, or say a new heart, maybe a new job or a car, maybe something else? Well by aligning ourselves with Christ, we can exercise our faith and see miracles pulled down from heaven as we are living out our heavenly position here on the earth.

Think of it like this. When we want to go somewhere, do we hop in a car and just sit there waiting for the vehicle to take us from point A to point B, without us taking any action? No of course not. We have to stick the key into the ignition and then turn the key, to get the engine going, and then we have to drive the vehicle from point A to point B. Faith operates just like a key does in relationship to a car. We have to put the key of faith in our Spirit and turn it to connect with Jesus.

When we need an answer to prayer, then we need to pull out the key of faith and turn towards heaven so the Lord can move into our situation. Remember faith without works is dead, so if we stand idle and do nothing, it's the same as approaching a car and not putting the key in the ignition. Faith is alive and active; it initiates a connection to God to get His reaction.

Chapter Two

The Measure of Faith

God in His loving and compassionate nature, so longs to have a close and intimate relationship with humanity that He has in His Divine wisdom, deposited a way in which we can participate and connect with Him while demonstrating His power. He accomplished this by depositing within us a Measure of Faith. In fact, the Spirit of God has deposited a measure of Himself in the manifestation of the gifts of the Spirit, one of which is this Measure of Faith.

1 Corinthians 12: 7 says:

"NOW TO EACH ONE THE MANIFESTATION OF THE SPIRIT IS GIVEN FOR THE COMMON GOOD. TO ONE THERE IS GIVEN THROUGH THE SPIRIT THE MESSAGE OF WISDOM, TO ANOTHER THE MESSAGE OF KNOWLEDGE BY MEANS OF THE SAME SPIRIT, **TO ANOTHER FAITH BY THE SAME SPIRIT**, TO ANOTHER GIFTS OF HEALING BY THAT ONE SPIRIT, TO ANOTHER MIRACULOUS POWERS, TO ANOTHER PROPHECY, TO ANOTHER DISTINGUISHING BETWEEN SPIRITS, TO ANOTHER SPEAKING IN DIFFERENT KINDS OF TONGUES, AND TO STILL ANOTHER THE INTERPRETATION OF TONGUES. ALL THESE ARE THE WORK OF ONE AND THE SAME SPIRIT, **AND HE GIVES THEM TO EACH ONE, JUST AS HE DETERMINES.**"

It says at the end of this verse that **He gives them to each one**; this can mean a measure of each gift has been given to each one of us. Why? Because if we are a believer and are filled with the Holy Spirit; then we can manifest any and all of the gifts, according to the measure of His choosing, at any given time, for His

Divine purpose. Some folks are given an extra ordinary measure of a particular gift, which they become more pronounced in, however each person who is baptized with the Holy Spirit and fire, has access to every gift according to the measure that has been given to them personally.

The amplified says it like this: "ALL OF THESE ACHIEVEMENTS AND ABILITIES ARE INSPIRED AND BROUGHT TO PASS BY ONE AND THE SAME HOLY SPIRIT, WHO APPORTIONS TO EACH PERSON INDIVIDUALLY, EXACTLY AS HE CHOOSES."

Now we need to remember that different gifts are needed for different situations and circumstances. Therefore the Spirit of God can manifest a gift at any time within an individual for His Divine purpose. However there are certain things that God deposits within every individual, the Gift of Faith is one of those things. We all need this in order to believe.

Romans 12:3 says:

"DO NOT THINK OF YOURSELF MORE HIGHLY THAN YOU OUGHT, BUT RATHER THINK OF YOURSELF WITH SOBER JUDGMENT, IN ACCORDANCE WITH THE **MEASURE OF FAITH** GOD HAS GIVEN YOU."

Ephesians 4:7 says:

"BUT UNTO EVERY ONE OF US IS GIVEN GRACE ACCORDING TO THE MEASURE OF THE GIFT OF CHRIST."

Every individual is given a unique Measure of Faith, at the Spirit's choosing. This Measure of Faith that each of us have is like a personalized seed. We can cultivate it and nurture it, and cause it to grow as the Spirit waters it. As I mentioned earlier, the Spirit gives the Measure of Faith as a gift, so it is yours, it will not be taken away from you. He personally deposited within you.

Nurturing faith can enable a person's faith to grow and mature even beyond a person who was given a larger Measure of Faith if that person did nothing to nurture it.

Think of the parable of talents or minas... A master was going on a journey and distributed among his servants these talents, one man was given one, and still another was given two and another five all according to their ability. The servant that had one talent did nothing profitable and buried it. The others went to work and double the original talents that were given, and were rewarded by their master. This is the same with everything God gives us including the measure of faith.

Jesus said in Luke 16:10

"WHOEVER CAN BE TRUSTED WITH VERY LITTLE CAN ALSO BE TRUSTED WITH MUCH, AND WHOEVER IS DISHONEST WITH VERY LITTLE WILL ALSO BE DISHONEST WITH MUCH."

Now there is also **EVER INCREASING** Gift of Faith. This is a bonus onto the original Measure of Faith that was given to you by God. Again this is a bonus gift, this is not something that can be earned, it is by His grace that it is given.

Now you can of course contend for the Ever Increasing Gift of Faith. We do this by seeking, asking and knocking, pushing, pressing and pursuing God both day and night with an expectation that we will receive something; and if nothing else, your measure of faith will mature and increase as a result of your efforts. That of course is the bottom line, that whatever measure of faith you are given; you are responsible to nurture that measure.

Now with this in mind let us take look at Matthew 17:20:

Jesus replied: "BECAUSE YOU HAVE SO LITTLE FAITH. I TELL YOU THE TRUTH, IF YOU HAVE FAITH AS SMALL AS A MUSTARD SEED, YOU CAN SAY TO THIS MOUNTAIN, 'MOVE FROM HERE TO THERE' AND IT WILL MOVE. NOTHING WILL BE IMPOSSIBLE FOR YOU."

Here Jesus reveals so much about the measure of faith by comparing faith to a seed. Seeds are meant to do what? *Be planted.* They are meant to be sown into good soil and nurtured to produce a harvest.

Jesus names the size of the disciple's faith; it was a **small** measure of faith; and up to that point, they had done nothing to further cultivate and nurture their faith, or cause it to mature.

If you give a farmer a bunch of seeds, do you think he is going to just sit on it? Of course not, he is going to sow it into good soil, water it and in today's age, put fertilizer on it.

Jesus is communicating to us that if we would cultivate and feed our faith, **even if our measure of faith is small**; that it can do crazy things, and NOTHING WILL BE IMPOSSIBLE FOR US.

The Measure of Faith is faith, which grows when we use it. This means that we need to have faith that is active, and will require us to actually step out and do something. Faith without works is dead (James 2:17).

Do you remember the analogy of the microchip? Microchips are only useful when they are programed and actually put to use, not boxed up in storage; but when they are put to use, even though they are small, they are extremely active.

Today microchips are being used to send massive amounts of money from nation to nation, information from state to state, operating our cell phones, fly our planes; they even put them in our cars now. Microchips and computers now run our daily sources of transportations; and if our faith is small like these tiny microchips, we can do even more powerful things than these.

One day, Jesus was walking and became hungry. He approached a fig tree and noticed that it had not bared fruit that was good to eat so he cursed the tree to death, and it immediately it withered to the disciple's amazement!

Then Jesus said in Matthew 21:21:

"I TELL YOU THE TRUTH, IF YOU HAVE FAITH AND DO NOT DOUBT, NOT ONLY CAN YOU DO WHAT WAS DONE TO THE FIG TREE, BUT ALSO YOU CAN SAY TO THIS MOUNTAIN, "GO, THROW YOURSELF INTO THE SEA, AND IT WILL BE DONE. IF YOU BELIEVE, YOU WILL RECEIVE WHATEVER YOU ASK FOR IN PRAYER."

Years ago when I was in Bible College, one of my professors said Jesus didn't actually mean that we could literally move mountains, but that the mountains Jesus spoke of were symbolic of difficult circumstances. I was shocked, and blurted out "What?" Moreover, he was surprised at my reaction. Then he asked me: "Well you don't actually believe that Jesus was really saying you can move literal mountains, like Mt. St Helens do you?" Conviction overcame me and I responded by saying: "Well, yes I think that is exactly what He is saying."

Now of course the mountains *can* be symbolic; the Holy Spirit can breathe on that verse for any individual regarding their circumstances. However, it also does not negate the fact that Jesus told us that we can move literal mountains in His name by faith. Remember, it is all in accordance to the measure of faith you have been given.

Let us look at this passage again, but this time starting with verse 18:

"AND HE LEFT THEM AND WENT OUT OF THE CITY TO BETHANY, WHERE HE SPENT THE NIGHT.

EARLY IN THE MORNING, AS HE WAS ON HIS WAY BACK TO THE CITY, HE WAS HUNGRY. SEEING A FIG TREE BY THE ROAD, HE WENT UP TO IT BUT FOUND NOTHING ON IT EXCEPT LEAVES. THEN HE SAID TO IT, "MAY YOU NEVER BEAR FRUIT AGAIN!" IMMEDIATELY THE TREE WITHERED.

WHEN THE DISCIPLES SAW THIS, THEY WERE AMAZED. "HOW DID THE FIG TREE WITHER SO QUICKLY?" THEY ASKED.

JESUS REPLIED, "I TELL YOU THE TRUTH, IF YOU HAVE FAITH AND DO NOT DOUBT, NOT ONLY CAN YOU DO WHAT WAS DONE TO THE FIG TREE, BUT ALSO YOU CAN SAY TO THIS MOUNTAIN, "GO, THROUGH YOURSELF INTO THE SEA, AND IT WILL BE DONE. IF YOU BELIEVE, YOU WILL RECEIVE WHATEVER YOU ASK FOR IN PRAYER."

Therefore, my position is yes, if Jesus curses the tree and it withers to death and then tells the disciples that we can say to this mountain "Go, throw yourself into the sea," then that is exactly what I believe will happen if I respond in faith.

Frankly, I don't understand why that is so hard to believe. Moses and Elijah parted the seas. Elijah called down fire from heaven; and Elisha performed twice as many miracles as Elijah. Our God is an amazing God, in fact, He is an awesome God.

Jesus said in John 14:12:

"ANYONE WHO HAS FAITH IN ME WILL DO GREATER THINGS THAN THESE.

Come on now, with God ALL things are possible. Everything is possible to him who believes. And if the Scriptures are true, and according to my faith it will be done, and I am full of faith by the Holy Spirit; I walk by faith and not by sight, knowing that life and death are in the power of the tongue, I can therefore speak what I hear from God, because faith comes by hearing and hearing by a Word from God; then I believe that I can say to any mountain move from here to there and it will be done.

This doesn't mean I go to every mountain and do some kind of weird chant, trying to move each mountain I can find. Faith is not witchcraft. Simon the sorcerer wanted to buy faith because he presumed it to be a power that could be purchased; not perceiving that it is actually a connection to the Living all powerful God.

Some people are power seekers. The pride of man desires to possess powers independent of God, to become their own source, their own god. Unfortunately

Christians often are power seekers, not realizing that they are missing the main ingredient: God. This is not the occult we are in but the Church.

Some folks claim they walk in faith but are actually walking in presumption. Years ago I was praying with another ministry. Their team had gathered to pray for a series of meetings we were going to be doing together. They needed a location to hold the meetings. Every week their team would come up with an idea of where to hold the meetings. Then they would name it and claim that location as if it was their own. They did this about four times before they discovered that one of the members of who was on their board of directors had some land they could use for the meetings. The lesson here is don't name and claim everything just because you want it.

Remember that faith is aligning into God, being plugged in, being linked into Him. God Himself is our power; He is our source of life. It is With GOD, ALL THINGS ARE POSSIBLE.

Remember Reinhard Bonnke said this:

"Faith is like a wiring system that carries power into our lives. The wiring system carries power but does not create power. Faith in of itself only carries power, but faith is not power, it only links us to the power source. However this is vital: there is no link to God without faith." [2]

Romans 10:17 says:

"CONSEQUENTLY, FAITH COMES FROM HEARING THE MESSAGE, AND THE MESSAGE IS HEARD THROUGH THE WORD OF CHRIST."

Christ is the Word and faith comes from hearing the Word, so let us keep on feeding the measure of faith that God has given us by meditating on God's spoken words over our life, such as any prophetic words we have received and by constant meditation of the Word of God that is alive and sharper than any two edged sword; for the Word of God when sent out, will do everything that it is sent to accomplish.

2

Chapter Three

The Gift of Faith

The Gift of faith is radically different than a measure of faith. The measure of faith is the original portion of faith God gives us individually.

The Gift of Faith however, is for the moment; the gift of faith is perfect, because it is the God kind of faith. It not only connects to God but also actually pulls on God, using His faith.

When the Gift of Faith is present, the supernatural overtakes the natural. The Gift of Faith believes for miracles and sees them materialize in the eyes of their spirit even before they materialize in the natural.

During the Healing Revival of the 1960's, William Branham, A.A. Allen, Oral Roberts and others moved and operated with The Gift of Faith.

If a man or woman operates in the moment with the God kind of faith, God's own faith, then they tap into Creator God. All things become possible. This brings a faith connection with God that heals the sick, performs miracles, signs and wonders and raises the dead.

I remember when I was first saved and went to my first revival conference. One night a granddaughter of AA Allen grabbed my brother and me and then took us to the altar to pray for someone. When we arrived there, she took us to a woman who was in a wheelchair and was weighing in over 400 pounds.

It took me a moment, but I recognized the woman in the wheelchair. As a newer believer, I was taking a Bible study class, and one of the women in the class was this lady's sister. Then it all hit me and I remembered the background story: the woman was paralyzed from the waist down from a car wreck that had occurred many years earlier.

However, AA Allen's granddaughter was not deterred by the obvious dubious circumstance; on the contrary, she was excited and praying up a storm. She became excited and continued to encourage my brother to pray. We did as she instructed and laid our hands on this 400 pound paralyzed woman; and then began to speak in tongues while AA Allen's granddaughter gets more and more excited; until it got to the point to where the woman in the wheelchair starts vibrating and then she jumps up and out of the wheelchair and takes off running.

I remember being in total amazement and turning my head towards my brother in total shock and watching him stair back at me with his jaw hanging out of his mouth. This was the first time I had experienced someone operating in The Gift of Faith.

In the mist of all the celebration, was a man that had a hand that was missing fingers. He saw what had just happened and he was moved. The Gift of Faith got on him, and his fingers started to grow and by the next day, he had five full-length fingers.

In this instance, AA Allen's granddaughter was operating in The Gift of Faith and then the man with the missing fingers caught it (the Gift of Faith), he believed for his hand, and he received his reward.

Sometimes The Gift of Faith comes from the person praying, other times it comes from someone interceding, and other times it could be the person who needs the healing.

A great example of this is the woman who touched the hem of Christ's garment. Jesus didn't seek out to heal that woman, yet she had faith that if she touched just the hem of His garment she would be healed. She was and immediately Jesus said, "Who touched me?"

After we prayed for that woman and she got out of that wheelchair, I thought that every person I prayed for that was stuck in a wheelchair was going to jump out completely healed. Others thought the same thing, so they sent me folks in wheelchairs, and I prayed for them, and I got no results. This caused confusion to me and for those who I prayed for.

The reason they were not healed was this: I was trying to see people healed and come out of wheelchairs by the measure of faith that was given to me. I was not operating in The Gift of Faith. I was trying to duplicate what I had seen. I saw a method and thought because I had been a part of the original group praying that I now had some extra ordinary gift of healing; however, I was missing the key ingredient, "*The Gift of Faith.*"

If someone does something in the supernatural through the Gift of Faith and you try to duplicate it with the measure of faith that God has pro-portioned to you then the miracle probably won't happen, because you're operating in a different kind of faith.

This could cause you to believe you have no faith, or weak pathetic faith, but you have to remember that the other person was moving and operating in The Gift of Faith. The Gift of Faith is for the moment; the gift of faith is perfect, the God kind of faith.

Jesus gave us an important, unforgettable lesson on The Gift of Faith in Mark 11. On a spring afternoon, Jesus and His disciples were traveling by foot across a dry desert when they came up to a fig tree. As they came closer, they noticed that the tree had withered from its roots. Peter remembered and said to Jesus, "RABBI, LOOK! THE FIG TREE YOU CURSED HAS WITHERED!"

JESUS ANSWERS BY SAYING: "HAVE THE FAITH OF GOD." Now many of your Bibles might say… "HAVE FAITH IN GOD" however that is a miss translation, a major grammatical error by the translators… and it creates some problems with the faith connection to God and this is why: Demons believe in God too and they shutter in fear of Him.

Imagine for a moment a person with cancer says: "I believe in God, I believe He can and is able to heal me, and I am hoping He will, but I don't KNOW IF HE WILL.

Do you see where that person just lost the faith connection? They don't *know* if He will heal them.

Let's read this verse correctly over again:

"HAVE THE FAITH OF GOD," JESUS ANSWERED. "I TELL YOU THE TRUTH, IF ANYONE SAYS TO THIS MOUNTAIN, 'GO THROW YOURSELF INTO THE SEA, AND DOES NOT DOUBT IN HIS HEART BUT BELIEVES THAT WHAT HE SAYS WILL HAPPEN, IT WILL BE DONE FOR HIM. THEREFORE I TELL YOU, WHATEVER YOU ASK FOR IN PRAYER, BELIEVE THAT YOU HAVE RECEIVED IT, AND IT WILL BE YOURS."

FRIENDS DO YOU KNOW WHAT THIS MEANS!!!!

The Gift of Faith is actually **God's Faith**. We can move into and operate in God's own faith, the faith of God. This means that we can actually move in and operate in Creator God, as in the Creator of the Universe kind of Faith. Life and death are in the power of the tongue… we can actually cause life and death to a fig tree.

When we tap into the God kind of faith, we are walking as one with Him and nothing is impossible, because we believe and are flowing in and with Him as His vessel!

We can command blind eyes to see, deaf ears to open, demons to flee, mountains to become a plain, darkness to become light, crooked places become straight. Skies can be shut up by our words, and we can walk on water; literally we can walk on water in the Gift of Faith, because all things are possible with God, and we are moving in and through His faith.

There is a compound interest to The Gift of Faith; a multiplying aspect to The Gift of Faith when it operates before large crowds who are present to its influence; because The Gift of Faith is tangible and transferable and can and probably will set or transform an entire atmosphere.

The Gift of Faith is catchable in fact it can be contagious. If you have ever been to a healing meeting where healings or miracles have taken place, then you have seen this.

One time when I was in Pakistan, I was teaching church leaders how to heal the sick. First I had them pray for the sick like normally would do and nothing happened. Then I transitioned to teach them about our authority in Christ and told them to command the sicknesses to go, when suddenly two teenage girls walked on to the stage, one of which was born deaf.

They approached my friend Hamilton who was seated behind me on the stage, and as I was teaching, Hamilton laid his hands on the deaf girl and commanded the deaf and dumb spirit to go and immediately her ears opened and she was healed.

This supercharged the atmosphere and supersized everyone's faith. Then I instructed the audience to do as Hamilton had just done on the stage. One by one they laid their hands on people of all kinds of sicknesses and diseases commanded the ailments to go and the result was awesome. Sixty two people were healed of their various ailments.

The Gift of faith does not see through the natural eyes, it sees through the eyes of God. This is possible because the faith connection by our spirit becomes one with God for that very moment.

God sees only possibilities; He does not stair at our circumstances and see uncertainty and He certainly does not see defeat. God only sees *triumphant victory.*

When The Gift of Faith is in operation, we operate with His faith, and thus see things with His eyes and understand His perspectives.

Let us look to Jesus as He operated in The Gift of Faith by turning with me to the book of John Chapter 11 starting with verse one:

"NOW A MAN NAMED LAZARUS WAS SICK. HE WAS FROM BETHANY, THE VILLAGE OF MARY AND HER SISTER MARTHA."

Verse three:

"SO THE SISTERS SENT WORD TO JESUS, "LORD, THE ONE YOU LOVE IS SICK." WHEN HE HEARD THIS, JESUS SAID, 'THIS SICKNESS WILL NOT END IN DEATH. NO, IT IS FOR GOD'S GLORY SO THAT GOD'S SON MAY BE GLORIFIED THROUGH IT.' JESUS LOVED MARTHA AND HER SISTER AND LAZARUS. YET WHEN HE HEARD THAT LAZARUS WAS SICK, HE STAYED WHERE HE WAS TWO MORE DAYS."

Then he said to his disciples, "LET US GO BACK TO JUDEA."

Verse 11:

"OUR FRIEND LAZARUS HAS FALLEN ASLEEP; BUT I AM GOING THERE TO WAKE HIM UP." HIS DISCIPLES REPLIED, "LORD, IF HE SLEEPS, HE WILL GET BETTER." JESUS HAD BEEN SPEAKING OF HIS DEATH, BUT HIS DISCIPLES THOUGHT HE MEANT NATURAL SLEEP. SO THEN HE TOLD THEM PLAINLY, "LAZARUS IS DEAD, AND FOR YOUR SAKE I AM GLAD I WAS NOT THERE, SO THAT YOU MAY BELIEVE. BUT LET US GO TO HIM."

Here we can see how Jesus truly sees the condition of his dear friend Lazarus. Though Lazarus was dead, Jesus saw him as asleep and needed to be awakened. Jesus was "*seeing*" through the eyes of The Gift of Faith.

The Gift of Faith allows us to see the end from the beginning, it can awaken us to see what God is going to accomplish in a given circumstance and situation.

We all know how the story ends. By the time Jesus gets there, Lazarus had been dead for three days, yet Jesus raises him from the dead. In addition, all those that had come to visit Mary and mourn Lazarus's death, witness the raising of the dead, causing many to put their faith in Him. This is how The Gift of Faith operates.

REMEMBER: There is the Measure of Faith, which we all have as individuals, and then there is The Gift of Faith which is for the moment; the gift of faith is perfect, the God kind of faith. It not only connects to God but also actually pulls on God, using His faith.

ALL of the power gifts, healings, miracles, signs and wonders find their origins with The Gift of Faith. It is the starting point of witnessing the impossible become possible, because with God all things are possible. Everything is possible for them who believe.

Chapter Four

The Prayer of Faith

The prayer of faith is a warring kind of faith. In other words, it is tenacious faith. It is faith that won't give up or give in not matter what. It doesn't matter what the circumstances look like, it doesn't matter what we feel like, it doesn't matter what others think; it's just faith that believes.

Turn with me to the book of James Chapter Five as we look at the prophet Elijah for a moment.

Starting with verse 17 it says:

"ELIJAH WAS A MAN JUST LIKE US. HE PRAYED EARNESTLY THAT IT WOULD NOT RAIN, AND IT DID NOT RAIN ON THE LAND FOR THREE AND A HALF YEARS. AGAIN HE PRAYED, AND THE HEAVENS GAVE RAIN AND THE EARTH PRODUCED ITS CROPS."

It says here that Elijah was *just like us*, and he *prayed earnestly that it would not rain*. What does this mean? This means that he prayed *fervently*.

The fervent prayer of a righteous man shall avail much because it is prayer that is not going to give in until it accomplishes victory; it means we will push, press, and pursue; we will seek, ask and knock; Contend again and again; constantly making our request known to God.

This means never giving up and letting go, but staying in that place of humility but knocking down every obstacle, throwing every demon to the ground, casting ever mountain into the sea, warring and contending for the breakthrough until we see the promise of God come to pass.

Do you want to see the deaf hear? Then pray for deaf people. However, if you're not operating with The Gift of Faith and nothing happens, don't stop there. No, keep on seeking, keep on asking, keep on knocking, push, press and pursue until you get your breakthrough and until The Gift of Faith arises so that the healing for the deaf and blind becomes a reality.

This can pertain to other matters in life as well. My wife and I needed breakthrough on a number of fronts, some of which involved attorneys and legal matters that were in the natural, out of our control. This didn't mean that I was going to sit on the sidelines and do nothing; we prayed and prayed again, until we saw the promises of God come to pass.

The Prayer of Faith is not a prayer that is just hopeful and laid back, no it goes for it. This is the kind of faith that has already moved mountains from the inside. You don't see the problems anymore, you only see breakthrough because you possess eyes of faith. You see the substance of things hoped for, you see the evidence of things not seen and you're hungry and passionately motivated to see this **all** the way through.

A great example of this is Kobe Bryant of the Lakers. As he played basketball, all he wanted to do was win. He would do anything, including playing basketball with broken fingers, bad knees, sprained ankles or a torn Achilles tendon. He would do anything and everything to get another championship; because he is possessed with the HEART & WILL of a champion.

The Prayer of Faith comes out of the Heart and WILL that is fixated on God for a single purpose. It is the heart of a champion that conquers until victory is accomplished. It is important to remember that faith is tied, it is connected to our will, and prayers that don't move you, won't move Him.

In 1 Kings 18 we see Elijah climb to the top of Mount Carmel, and he bends down to the ground and puts his face between his knees and he begins to labor in prayer.

When Elijah's servant comes to him, he sends the servant to look towards the sea, and the servant turns back and tells Elijah, "THERE IS NOTHING THERE." This goes on **SEVEN** times. Elijah stayed in this position and fervently prayed the prayer of faith until the SEVENTH time Elijah said, go back, and look at the sea. It was only on the seventh time that the servant reported to his master Elijah "I SEE THE CLOUD THE SIZE OF A MAN'S HAND."

That is the example by which the Book of James is calling the Prayer of Faith. The kind of prayer that is going to pray and pray until the breakthrough comes to pass because by faith we are positioned to see the breakthrough.

The Prayer of Faith is a place of posturing, a place of positioning, by aligning yourself to God and through the vehicle of prayer connecting with Christ to see something breakthrough. It is a place of intense faith filled intercession that proves to be effective.

Years ago when I was in Bible College, I arrived early to our required Chapel service. I was the second person there… and I noticed the man preparing the sound system was struggling; he was limping badly. Therefore, I asked him if he had a sprained ankle, which he obviously did, so he said "yes" …. When I sat down I asked if I could pray for him. He came over and just threw his foot right in my lap, very a matter of fact like. At that point, I was not going to pray some lazy prayer; I prayed the Prayer of Faith and commanded that ankle to be healed.

When I commanded healing to his ankle, he felt faith arise in his heart, and mentioned that he thought something might be happening to his ankle. As he realized this possibility, his entire facial expression changed and was full of joy and obvious expectation.

Then people arrived and the service started, the worship music was going, so I figured his work must be about done, so I went back over to him and asked him how his ankle was, and he acknowledged there had been a little improvement.

Some people stop with that and have a party, celebrating, and giving testimonies about a 10% healing. I knew he was filled with faith and was greatly encouraged before, but I was full of the Prayer of Faith, I wanted more. So I laid hands on him again and commanded more healin; then I grabbed his arm, and I dragged him up and down the chapel several times. I tried to get him to speed walk so he wouldn't have time to mentally process what was going on with his ankle.

At first he stumbled as he thought of the pain, but I would have none of that, so again I pushed him through it to look at God and not at the circumstance he was in.

A doctor would have freaked out if they saw the way I had been pushing him. Most people in that situation will get overwhelmed by the symptoms and will give in to the pain; I didn't allow this man to do that. I dragged him up and down that chapel for the next five to seven minutes until the seed of faith that had been planted in his heart would germinate into a full blow one hundred percent healing.

Then he decided to take off his ankle wrappings, so I asked him if it hurt. His response was perfect, he shook off the pain and started stomping his foot vigorously, again and again. Then he started jumping on both feet and eventually walked up and down that chapel, this time without me and praised God. At this point, the entire audience at the services was watching in amazement.

Let me tell you, this guy caught it, he walked in faith. Every time I saw him from then on, he remembered that experience of faith and victory in his life.

The prayer of faith is tenacious. It doesn't back down, give up, or let up, won't bow to the circumstance or emotions that surround it, because it sees with the eyes of faith.

Do you want your God given inheritance, then pray, pray and pray the prayer of faith until you get your breakthrough; keep on contending, don't back down. Keep on seeking, keep and asking, keep on knocking on the doors of heaven until you get your breakthrough.

It doesn't matter if you're worn out, it doesn't matter if you are tired and beaten down. The prayer of faith is not a matter of emotions, it is something tangible from your spirit where you take control of your thoughts and emotions and make them think and feel the way God needs them to think and feel in order to get the breakthrough.

Right now for all of those reading this, I pray:

Father cause hearts to burn with the intensity of a champion, send angels to drop hot fiery coals from heaven into their hearts to burn hotter for Jesus and cause the wind of the Spirit to blow in and through them as they begin to pray the Prayer of Faith. Awaken a thirst and a hunger that is never easily satisfied to pierce their hearts so they will push, press and pursue, seek, ask and knock until the breakthrough is theirs. Lord, awaken the overcomers; awaken "Your" champions!

Jesus, open our eyes to see how it is we are to war and contend by faith in the Spirit for healings and miracles and to throw out unbelief and take possession of the promises of God that are ours. In Jesus name so be it, Amen!

Chapter Five

Revelation Faith

Revelation Faith has eyes that see and ears that hear in the Spirit; then takes action by demonstrating what was seen and heard. This is the kind of spiritual faith which receives downloads from the Holy Spirit and responds accordingly.

A key component to operating in this kind of faith is to fix our eyes on things above (heaven), and not on things below (natural), Colossians 3:2. This might sound spiritual, even unnatural. In fact, you might have heard the expression: *"So heavenly minded that you are of no earthly good."* That is a lie from the pit of hell (Romans 8:5-6).

The reality is we are called to be heavenly minded so we **can** be of some earthly good. We are to leave a Divine imprint of His Kingdom in this world. We are children of heaven on this earth, and are to be led in the Spirit, just like Jesus was led by our Heavenly Father.

John 5:19-21 says:

"I TELL YOU THE TRUTH, THE SON CAN DO NOTHING BY HIMSELF; HE CAN DO ONLY WHAT HE SEES HIS FATHER DOING, BECAUSE WHATEVER THE FATHER DOES THE SON ALSO DOES. FOR THE FATHER LOVES THE SON AND SHOWS HIM ALL HE DOES.

Jesus Himself operated in this kind of faith. Jesus only did as He saw His Father do. How could this be? Jesus spent time in the secret place, listening and watching the Father in prayer. In other words, Jesus fellowshipped with the Father; and during those intimate encounters the Son received prophetic downloads which He then acted upon when He encountered the multitudes of sick people; because He already had seen what the Father was doing among them.

This is where faith comes into a revelatory form; where a prophetic platform is established for operating in the Gift of Faith. It is here; the Holy Spirit speaks or illuminates a revelation that we are, in turn, to act out.

Revelation Faith could also be called **Rhema Faith**. The word "*rhema*" is a Greek word that refers to the "*Spoken Word*" where the Holy Spirit speaks directly to us; whereas the Greek word "*logos*" is referred to as the "*Written Word*" of God (Scripture).

Romans 10:17 says: FAITH COMES BY HEARING, AND HEARING BY THE WORD OF GOD.

The Measure of Faith is strengthened and grows by reading and hearing the "*Written Word*" of God; however Revelation Faith comes by hearing "*A Spoken Word*" of God. It is Divine inspired revelation.

In Revelation Faith, God speaks to us and then we are to act out what God has revealed to us by His Spirit. The entire earthly ministry of Jesus was premeditated on this kind of faith. Remember, the Son only did what He saw His Father doing.

Jesus said in John 15:7:

IF YOU REMAIN IN ME AND MY WORDS REMAIN IN YOU, ASK WHATEVER YOU WISH, AND IT WILL BE DONE FOR YOU.

Spending time in the Secret Place; time alone with God is *key;* it is paramount to entering into this kind of faith. We must continually abide in the Vine, for a branch (you) cannot survive unless it abides in the Vine (Christ). We must continually position and posture ourselves in a place of waiting on God and allowing the words that He speaks to us, to remain within us. This requires coming into rest.

The rest of God is a place of abiding; soaking in His presence, and listening to Him without giving Him a list of prayer requests. We are to literally wait, and cause our soul to be still (mind, will and emotions). This takes time and practice to develop; however this is crucial to receiving revelation because God's voice is not like the noise in the world.

Everything around us is loud and brings clutter and confusion. God however communicates with a soft voice; which requires quietness in order to hear. This is why Jesus spent time alone with the Father; away from not only the crowds by even the disciples.

Matthew 14:23 says:
AFTER HE HAD DISMISSED THEM, HE WENT UP ON A MOUNTAINSIDE BY HIMSELF TO PRAY. WHEN EVENING CAME, HE WAS THERE ALONE.

Luke 6:12 says:
ONE OF THOSE DAYS JESUS WENT OUT TO A MOUNTAINSIDE TO PRAY, AND SPENT THE NIGHT PRAYING TO GOD.

This is why Jesus was able to say in John 5:19-21: "I TELL YOU THE TRUTH, THE SON CAN DO NOTHING BY HIMSELF; HE CAN DO ONLY WHAT HE SEES HIS FATHER DOING, BECAUSE WHATEVER THE FATHER DOES THE SON ALSO DOES. FOR THE FATHER LOVES THE SON AND **SHOWS** HIM ALL HE DOES.

Because Jesus spent time in the Secret Place, He received fresh revelation which became a blueprint for actionable faith. He waited, listened, and saw until He received Revelation Faith. Then He applied what He received by performing great demonstrations of power that produced fruit.

A great example of when Jesus did this very thing is found in Matthew 14:22-25:

IMMEDIATELY JESUS MADE THE DISCIPLES GET INTO THE BOAT AND GO ON AHEAD OF HIM TO THE OTHER SIDE, WHILE HE DISMISSED THE CROWD. AFTER HE HAD DISMISSED THEM, **HE WENT UP ON A MOUNTAINSIDE BY HIMSELF TO PRAY.** WHEN EVENING CAME, **HE WAS THERE ALONE,** BUT THE BOAT WAS ALREADY A CONSIDERABLE

DISTANCE FROM LAND, BUFFETED BY THE WAVES BECAUSE THE WIND WAS AGAINST IT. DURING THE FOURTH WATCH OF THE NIGHT, JESUS WENT OUT TO THEM, **WALKING ON THE LAKE**.

Here Jesus made a point to have time in the Secret Place, where He was alone with His Father. Jesus came away from that encounter by walking in Revelation Faith, which He then demonstrated in miraculous fashion: Walking on Water!

The disciples are both terrified and amazed. Peter is initially inspired and tries to walk on the water too; however he is influenced by his natural surroundings and sinks. Jesus of course takes Peter's hand and says to Peter: "YOU OF LITTLE FAITH... WHY DID YOU DOUBT?"

Through the centuries, this portion of Scripture has been used to illustrate faith because of its tremendous insight. For one, Peter was spending all of his time with the other disciples and not alone with the Father; thus he had not received fresh revelation of what the Father was doing. Peter was bold for getting out of the boat and onto the water; however his eyes were not on things above but upon his surroundings.

Peter learns his lesson, in Acts chapter ten, he climbs to a roof to pray. During his time with God, he falls into a trance; and God reveals a mystery to him. When Peter awakens, the Spirit says to him: "SIMON, THREE MEN (Foreigners) ARE LOOKING FOR YOU. SO GET

UP AND GO DOWNSTAIRS. DO NOT HESITATE TO GO WITH THEM, FOR I HAVE SENT THEM."

Jesus then reveals to Peter that the God does not show favoritism but accepts men from every nation that fear God and do what is right. Peter would not have had the faith to believe for this if he had not first been in the Secret Place, waiting on God.

Revelation Faith comes from a place of receiving from God, not a place of our own understanding or by our own works. Striving and trying to work something up is useless here. In Revelation Faith, we receive the Spirit of wisdom and revelation (Ephesians 2) so that we can know God, having our eyes enlightened in order that we may know the hope to which He calls us into; so that we can see God is His fullness and then do what He is doing.

Understanding the reality of **who** abides within us is crucial as we operate in Revelation Faith. Remember, greater is Christ that is in you, than the demons in the world; that you can do ALL things through Christ who gives you strength.

Some people try to cleanse the atmosphere and open the heavens so that God can move. In truth, they are creating an environment to satisfy their comfort zone because of their unbelief.

We can do ministry anywhere, after all: Jesus Himself is an open heaven. If you are truly abiding in Him and He is in you, and if you are doing as you see our Heavenly Father doing, then God's going to be reveal His power.

John 1:51 says:

"I TELL YOU THE TRUTH, YOU WILL SEE 'HEAVEN OPEN, AND THE ANGELS OF GOD ASCENDING AND DESCENDING ON THE SON OF MAN."

Again, Jesus is the open heaven, with angels ascending and descending upon Him; and He is living inside of YOU. We have the God of the universe living inside of us and He wants to communicate with us regarding what He is doing. By stepping into the revelation which He gives, we can operate in a level of faith that is truly supernatural.

Practical Tools & Application

1. Commit time in the Secret Place with God.
    a. Wait
    b. Listen
    c. See
    d. Write down what He reveals

2. Begin each day with a faith picture (in your mind) of what He revealed to you in the Secret Place and what you see Him doing.
    a. Expect that God is going to continue speak & reveal things throughout the day

3. Declare, confess and pray into what God reveals in the Secret Place.
    a.

4. Act! Demonstrate and follow through with what God has revealed to you in secrete.

Chapter Six

The Faith of a Centurion

Let us examine the Roman Centurion in Gospel of Matthew 8:5-13:

5 WHEN JESUS HAD ENTERED CAPERNAUM, A
CENTURION CAME TO HIM, ASKING FOR HELP. 6 "LORD,"
HE SAID, "MY SERVANT LIES AT HOME PARALYZED,
SUFFERING TERRIBLY."

7 JESUS SAID TO HIM, "I WILL COME AND HEAL HIM"

8 THE CENTURION REPLIED, "LORD, I DO NOT DESERVE
TO HAVE YOU COME UNDER MY ROOF. BUT JUST SAY THE
WORD, AND MY SERVANT WILL BE HEALED. 9 FOR I
MYSELF AM A MAN UNDER AUTHORITY, WITH SOLDIERS
UNDER ME. I TELL THIS ONE, 'GO,' AND HE GOES; AND
THAT ONE, 'COME,' AND HE COMES. I SAY TO MY
SERVANT, 'DO THIS,' AND HE DOES IT."

10 WHEN JESUS HEARD THIS, HE WAS AMAZED AND SAID
TO THOSE FOLLOWING HIM, "TRULY I TELL YOU, I HAVE
NOT FOUND ANYONE IN ISRAEL WITH SUCH GREAT FAITH.
11 I SAY TO YOU THAT MANY WILL COME FROM THE EAST
AND THE WEST, AND WILL TAKE THEIR PLACES AT THE
FEAST WITH ABRAHAM, ISAAC AND JACOB IN THE
KINGDOM OF HEAVEN. 12 BUT THE SUBJECTS OF THE
KINGDOM WILL BE THROWN OUTSIDE, INTO THE
DARKNESS, WHERE THERE WILL BE WEEPING AND
GNASHING OF TEETH."

13 THEN JESUS SAID TO THE CENTURION, "GO! LET IT BE
DONE JUST AS YOU BELIEVED IT WOULD." AND HIS
SERVANT WAS HEALED AT THAT MOMENT.

There are only two times in all four Gospels that Jesus was amazed, and this is one of them.

The humanity of Jesus was amazed; in fact, He was moved and astonished by the great faith of the

Centurion Soldier. For starters, the Centurion Soldier knew his place, and he recognized who Jesus was and His place as the King of Kings.

Historically a Centurion Soldier was given charge over 100 soldiers that were to follow his command, which he received from an even higher-ranking officer.

Therefore, when the Centurion Soldier heard a command from one of his superiors, he directed it to his men accordingly. This is how a military operates and functions; each man having a rank of position. Not every man can be a chief, not every man can be the boss, there has to be someone who gives the orders and others that carry out those orders.

Jesus Himself said a house divided against itself cannot stand. The entire Kingdom of God operates in this kind of order.

When Jesus entered Capernaum and the centurion witnessed the authority Jesus operated in, he recognized that Jesus had authority greater than even Rome.

The Centurion Soldier recognized Jesus was the Christ Divine who could heal all sickness and disease. Therefore, he approached Jesus in humility but not ignorance. We know that because the Centurion Soldier refers to Jesus as "Lord," which is something Romans would not have attributed to Him at that time.

The Jewish nation was under Roman rule, under their occupation. Yet the Roman soldier calls Jesus "LORD," acknowledging Jesus as King of all Kings. Then he makes a plea for Jesus to help his servant who is suffering terribly and is paralyzed.

Another remarkable thing, how many Roman Military Commanders do you think possessed this kind of compassion? Keep in mind he is a soldier of a Roman military; and military's are made for war; he is by all means a warrior, he is a man's man that fights to the death, and he is there as an occupier.

Yet when Jesus arrives in town, this Commander is concerned for one of his men, and humbles himself before the King of another Kingdom, making a plea for Jesus to help someone under his command.

If we look at what the Centurion Soldier says, he never actually asks the question: "*Will you come and heal him*?" knowing that he didn't have that right. He was a Roman, and therefore not part of the Abrahamic Covenant. Yet he simply mentions to Jesus that he has a servant that was suffering.

Jesus immediately says that he will go and heal him. Why? Because the Centurion Soldiers faith has already moved Jesus into action and then the Centurion says something so profound it amazes even Jesus.

While the religious leaders of the day were skeptical and critical of their own Messiah, full of doubt and jealousy, the Centurion Soldier says this:

"LORD, I DO NOT DESERVE TO HAVE YOU COME UNDER MY ROOF. BUT JUST SAY THE WORD, AND MY SERVANT WILL BE HEALED. FOR I MYSELF AM A MAN UNDER AUTHORITY, WITH SOLDIERS UNDER ME. I TELL THIS ONE, 'GO,' AND HE GOES; AND THAT ONE, 'COME,' AND HE COMES. I SAY TO MY SERVANT, 'DO THIS,' AND HE DOES IT."

The Centurion Soldier understood faith because he understood authority. The Centurion Soldier had authority because he himself was under authority. Friends do you want authority. You must first be under authority. That's how it works.

Again, the Centurion Soldier was under authority and he had a place of authority, when he gave a command and set it in motion, everyone underneath him carried out that task. The spirit realm operates in this very manner. The Centurion Soldier recognized that Jesus was from above and had the authority of all of heaven.

He also recognized himself as unworthy to have Jesus in his home. The most personal and intimate way to interact with people socially in that culture and frankly most cultures today, is to have them in your home. But this soldier knew he was unworthy of such an honor.

When the Centurion Soldier says: "LORD, I DO NOT DESERVE TO HAVE YOU COME UNDER MY ROOF." He recognizes Jesus for who He is.

Yet the soldier recognizes that he is unworthy of the King of Kings. Jesus Christ is the King of the Kingdom, the King's domain, which of course is a higher kingdom than that of Rome.

He knew that Jesus was Christ and that Jesus had the ability to JUST SAY THE WORD and something supernatural would happen in the Spirit and enter into his lower ranking officer's body, bringing life and health into that mortal flesh.

There was no doubt or double minded thinking in the Centurions Soldiers mind. He simply said: "JUST SAY THE WORD."

How many times have we gotten a prophetic word and then needed another one so we could believe the first one God gave us? Here this man who is not even part of the Abrahamic Covenant, and says: "*Just say the Word and I believe, I know it will be, because I know the authority that you possess will carry it through.*"

Jesus then goes on to tell everyone: "TRULY I TELL YOU, I HAVE NOT FOUND ANYONE IN ISRAEL WITH SUCH GREAT FAITH. I SAY TO YOU THAT MANY WILL COME FROM THE EAST AND THE WEST, AND WILL TAKE THEIR PLACES AT THE FEAST WITH ABRAHAM, ISAAC AND JACOB IN THE KINGDOM OF HEAVEN. BUT THE SUBJECTS OF THE

KINGDOM WILL BE THROWN OUTSIDE, INTO THE DARKNESS, WHERE THERE WILL BE WEEPING AND GNASHING OF TEETH."

Church this is a warning. Many will want to take their place, saying, oh I went to church, oh I was part of this and that, oh I preached here and there, I healed the sick, I am a Christian, I am a good person, yet if He doesn't know you, WATCH OUT !!!

There are many so-called "unbelievers" out there that have more faith and would recognize Jesus and give Him more honor in humility than some people in the Church today.

Understanding rank and place are key components to understanding how faith operates in the Kingdom of God. We must understand our place and position in His kingdom. Jesus is the King of the entire Kingdom and we must recognize Him for who He is in all humility and recognize that His Words are final and true.

Jesus says you are healed, then there is no room to doubt, you are healed. Jesus says you broke-through then you broke-through. Jesus says you a free; then whom the Son sets free is indeed free. God honors His Word… for His Word is true.

Jesus said that the Centurion Soldier had great faith; he did because he understood authority, rank and position.

Do we as the Church recognize Christ as Master, and do we obey His Word? Do we submit to Him and do we carry out His commands? There is no great faith in rebellion, only in submission and understanding our place to Him and the Body.

If we want the wind, skies, and seas to obey us, and if we want to have dominion over demons, sickness, and death, then we need to obey Him and walk in His ways.

Chapter Seven

Unbelief

It is important for me to cover the topic of unbelief because it is the opposition and literally the exact opposite of faith.

Romans 14:23 says: "EVERYTHING THAT DOES NOT COME FROM FAITH IS SIN."

Hebrews 11:6 says: "WITHOUT FAITH IT IS IMPOSSIBLE TO PLEASE GOD."

Do I really need to say much more? Unbelief is wicked. Don't even entertain such thoughts, because what you tolerate will dominate.

Unbelief can take on many forms, including: doubting, being critical, cynical, skeptical, dignified, and full of self-reasoning. It asks questions God is not answering and is full of self-justification.

Unbelief is safe because it takes no risk and gets exactly what it expects. It is sad because unbelief is actually faith in something other than God. It's faith in another god.

Romans 1:25 says: "THEY EXCHANGED THE TRUTH ABOUT GOD FOR A LIE, AND WORSHIPED AND SERVED CREATED THINGS RATHER THAN THE CREATOR."

This is what unbelief does: it exchanges the truth for a lie. In the previous chapter, I mentioned that there were; only two times that Jesus was amazed in all four Gospels. In chapter six I mentioned that Jesus was amazed by the Roman Soldiers faith. The other time Jesus was amazed was by someone's lack of faith.

Mark 6:1:

"JESUS LEFT THERE AND WENT TO HIS HOMETOWN, ACCOMPANIED BY HIS DISCIPLES. WHEN THE SABBATH CAME, HE BEGAN TO TEACH IN THE SYNAGOGUE, AND MANY WHO HEARD HIM WERE AMAZED.

"**WHERE DID THIS MAN GET THESE THINGS**?" THEY ASKED. "WHAT'S THIS WISDOM THAT HAS BEEN GIVEN HIM? WHAT ARE THESE REMARKABLE MIRACLES HE IS PERFORMING? ISN'T THIS THE CARPENTER? ISN'T THIS MARY'S SON AND THE BROTHER OF JAMES, JOSEPH, JUDAS AND SIMON? AREN'T HIS SISTERS HERE WITH US?" **AND THEY TOOK OFFENSE AT HIM**."

A couple of verses later it says: "JESUS COULD NOT DO ANY MIRACLES THERE, EXCEPT LAY HIS HANDS ON A FEW SICK PEOPLE AND HEAL THEM. HE WAS **AMAZED** AT THEIR LACK OF FAITH."

This is the second time in scripture that Jesus in His humanity was amazed, and it was due to their unbelief.

Unbelief is usually offended at the package. They were bickering at the vessel that stood before them. The people were so familiar with Jesus and His family that they took offense at Him and thus, refused to receive what God had pre-ordained for them to receive!

This still happens today. Our ministry (Hearts of Fire International) has hosted several healing and miracle services, and we have seen God perform amazing wonders, only to have others including pastors reject either me or one of the other vessels (guest speakers) I brought in that God was using. It's always because they reject the package. When this happens, they also reject everything else God is doing.

Looking back at the verse, it says, "HE COULD NOT DO ANY MIRACLES THERE"; all he could do was lay His hands on a few sick people, *but He could do no miracles*. This should communicate the importance of faith. Jesus Christ Himself was not able to perform miracles in a location that didn't have faith. Unbelief at best has no expectation, it flat-lines.

Hebrews 11:6 says: "BUT WITHOUT FAITH IT IS IMPOSSIBLE TO PLEASE HIM; FOR THE PERSON THAT COMES TO GOD MUST BELIEVE THAT HE IS, AND THAT HE IS A REWARDER OF THEM THAT DILIGENTLY SEEK HIM."

If you remember earlier in the book I defined faith in this simple term, "*Faith is being plugged into God; it is the plugging in that is faith.*" When people are offended, it is as though they are an electric cord that is all bent out of shape; and the plug despises the plugin socket; it rejects the power source, refusing to be plugged in.

This is why offense is such big issue for many people who need healing. The medical field has proven that offense causes cancer. If people don't let go of offense their bodies get toxic. Offense and unbelief can actually *make* your body sick.

There is an incredible link between faith and trust and if people don't trust but are offended and despise the vessel or even the source of power (God) then nothing will happen. We are not to judge God or the vessels of His choosing that He is using.

Hebrews 10:38 says: "BUT MY RIGHTEOUS ONE SHALL LIVE BY FAITH; AND IF HE SHRINKS BACK, MY SOUL HAS NO PLEASURE IN HIM."

The Israelites witnessed God deliver them from the hands of Egypt through plagues and parting the Red Sea, but they began to whine and complain because they forgot the greatness of their God and stopped trusting in Him to be their everything; and started putting limits on God. They started boxing God in.

Psalm 78:41 says: "AGAIN AND AGAIN THEY PUT GOD TO THE TEST; THEY VEXED THE HOLY ONE OF ISRAEL."

Unbelief has a vexing power. It's like a giant spider storming in the room and spraying webs over everyone and everything until no one can move.

Think about this for a moment. How many readers out there know that indifference can settle after 38 years with no breakthrough? In the book of John chapter five, Jesus approaches a man who had been an invalid for 38 years!

This invalid had been hanging around a pool named Bethesda. Now from time to time an angel would come and heal whoever was in the pool, yet this man, for the last 38 years, had never made it in the pool at the right time.

Others were healed in those waters, but he wasn't. Just like so many of you reading this that have gone to healing meetings and seen others healed, when you were hoping and praying, but you yourself, went home empty. This man never received his healing, he could only look on as others; one after the other were healed instead of him.

He was still an invalid. His expectations at this point were low. We could even say that his expectation had flat-lined. He saw others healed in that pool, but disappointment after disappointment, this man had mostly given up.

Yet when Jesus hears about this invalid's condition, Jesus asks him the question "DO YOU WANT TO GET WELL"? In addition, the person proceeds to talk about why he can't be healed and then about all of the disappointments of the past.

Jesus hears the need but ignores the limitations the guy has put on himself. "I can't because, it won't happen cause; oh this has to happen first…"

Have you ever been around someone that never stops talking about all the obstacles and hardships they are going through; it is as if they are addicted to the process that makes them miserable.

It's like the old saying: "Misery loves company." In this case, they desire your company. You're the audience. They parade their struggles as if they are on a tour, reaching out to all their fans. It is disgusting. These people are so consumed with the obstacles that they have become disconnected from God, and have become a ball of yarn all tangled up.

Proverbs 12:18 says: "RECKLESS WORDS PIERCE LIKE A SWORD BUT THE TONGUE OF THE WISE BRINGS HEALING."

Let me give you a solid piece of advice: Don't let them ramble on. Jesus simply says "GET UP! PICK UP YOUR MAT AND WALK." The Bible says: "AT ONCE THE MAN WAS CURED; HE PICKED UP HIS MAT AND WALKED."

If faith is plugging into God, we can't let our circumstances, the pain, the failure, dictate to us our faith expectation; or else hoped differed will make our heart sick; which leaves us vulnerable and susceptible to being disconnected with God and run the risk of becoming hard of heart.

Matthew12:22 says:

"THEN THEY BROUGHT HIM A DEMON POSSESSED MAN WHO WAS BLIND AND MUTE, AND JESUS HEALED HIM, SO THAT HE COULD BOTH TALK AND SEE. ALL THE PEOPLE WERE ASTONISHED AND SAID, "COULD THIS BE THE SON OF DAVID?"

BUT WHEN THE PHARISEES HEARD THIS, THEY SAID, "IT IS ONLY BY BEELZEBUB, THE PRINCE OF DEMONS THAT THIS FELLOW DRIVES OUT DEMONS."

The religious leaders of the day were so filled with unbelief and offense that they said it is only by Beelzebub the Prince of Demons that he drives out demons.

Then in verse 38 they asked him this question: "TEACHER WE WANT TO SEE A MIRACULOUS SIGN FROM YOU." All I have to say about that is: "Whhhhaaatttt?"

Jesus just cast out demons from this man who was both blind and mute, bringing forth healing and they are asking for a sign?!

Unbelief is blind. Having eyes but not able to see. It is like an electric cord that is cut in half, the connection is broken. Unbelief questions even God.

Here Jesus is going around healing the sick, casting out demons, turning water into wine, feeding thousands with a single loaf of bread, and they are asking for a sign.

Ultimately, all sin is rooted in pride, including unbelief.

John 10:24 says: "THE JEWS GATHERED AROUND HIM, SAYING, "HOW LONG WILL YOU KEEP US IN SUSPENSE? IF YOU ARE THE CHRIST, TELL US PLAINLY." JESUS ANSWERED, "I DID TELL YOU, BUT YOU DID NOT BELIEVE. THE MIRACLES I DO IN MY FATHER'S NAME SPEAK FOR ME, BUT YOU DO NOT BELIEVE BECAUSE YOU ARE NOT MY SHEEP. MY SHEEP HEAR MY VOICE; I KNOW THEM, AND THEY FOLLOW ME."

The religious leaders didn't know God personally and were unable to hear His voice and recognize miracles right in front of their face because the effects of pride and unbelief blinded them.

In Mark chapter 9 a man brings Jesus his son and says, "IF YOU CAN DO ANYTHING, TAKE PITY ON HIM."

Jesus said: "IF I CAN?" He was appalled by this father's unbelief. The man was immediately humbled and replied: "I DO BELIEVE; HELP ME OVERCOME MY UNBELIEF!"

I love how this man makes the decision to throw out unbelief and cry out to Christ for mercy. However, he was still not speaking faith. Demons believe too, but they are not walking in faith. The Bible says out of the heart the mouth speaks, therefore we need to be careful what we say and what we come into agreement with. Sometimes what we confess or what someone else is saying about us is not full of faith but full of unbelief.

When I was 11years old, I started to have spine problems and by the age of 14 I had to have surgery to prevent me from being paralyzed. To this day, I have had to fight and contend for complete wholeness. Let me tell you, there have been days, weeks and even months that I have struggled for peace in this flesh of mine.

Through the years, I have come across people that have seen me struggling to walk and they say some of the most ignorant things like: "bad back huh" or "move over cripple." They speak with what their eyes see, they speak with unbelief, and they are blinded in the spirit realm by darkness. With their words, they tried to label me.

I have to tell you that I absolutely hate it when people say those kinds of things about me. I refuse to be in that condition, I have prayed the Prayer of Faith, had others have Prayed the Prayer of Faith; I have confessed the healing scriptures, and I have changed my diet, taken supplements, I workout and perform exercises that are specific for the injury as best my schedule allows, because I refuse to live the rest of my life as a cripple.

Today, because of my actions, I live a normal life. I have not let the words of others stick on me. Words of unbelief come from everyone imaginable: Doctors, family members, coworkers, friends, customers, and strangers. Do not let words of unbelief stick on you.

Don't let other define you. If your doctor speaks unbelief then change doctor.

I have done meetings all over the world with all kinds of groups, but if unbelief is really pronounced, I'll just walk away. If there is an abundance pride and control, then the people will not hear the Truth but believe a lie because it is more comfortable.

Do you remember what I said earlier? Unbelief is safe because it takes no risk and gets exactly what it expects. It is sad because unbelief is actually faith in something other than God.

Fear often looks like wisdom to those in **unbelief.** Unbelief doubts, it questions, is critical, cynical, skeptical, it is dignified and full of self -reason and full of self-righteousness and justification.

Unbelief doesn't want God to move, it resist Him. Know that if you allow this in your life: What you tolerate will dominate.

Revelations 21:8 says: "BUT THE COWARDLY, THE UNBELIEVING, THE VILE, THE MURDERERS, THE SEXUALLY IMMORAL, THOSE WHO PRACTICE MAGIC ARTS, THE IDOLATERS AND ALL LIARS – THEIR PLACE WILL BE IN THE FIERY LAKE OF BURNING SULFUR."

Romans 14:23 says: "EVERYTHING THAT DOES NOT COME FROM FAITH IS SIN."

Hebrews 11:6 says: "WITHOUT FAITH IT IS IMPOSSIBLE TO PLEASE GOD."

Until now, the kingdom of heaven suffers violence, and the violent take it by force. Do you want to know what to do with unbelief? Throw it out! Have dominion over unbelief. Rule over unbelief like a bug under your feet. Dominate it with faith-filled words. Celebrate God and His goodness with praise and thanksgiving.

Remember, this is the day that the Lord has made, rejoice and be glad in it. Our God is an awesome God and the Devil is a liar. Take the keys that Christ has given you to bind up and loosen. Lay hold of faith which is a substance of things hoped for, evidence of things not seen, because we walk by faith and not by sight.

Chapter Eight

The Faith of a Canaanite Woman

Turn with me to the book of Matthew chapter 15 starting with verse 21: LEAVING THAT PLACE, JESUS WITHDREW TO THE REGION OF TYRE AND SIDON. A CANAANITE WOMAN FROM THAT VICINITY CAME TO HIM, CRYING OUT, "LORD, SON OF DAVID, HAVE MERCY ON ME! MY DAUGHTER IS SUFFERING TERRIBLY FROM DEMON-POSSESSION." JESUS DID NOT ANSWER A WORD. SO HIS DISCIPLES CAME TO HIM AND URGED HIM, "SEND HER AWAY, FOR SHE KEEPS CRYING OUT AFTER US." HE ANSWERED, "I WAS SENT ONLY TO THE LOST SHEEP OF ISRAEL." THE WOMAN CAME AND KNELT BEFORE HIM. "LORD, HELP ME!" SHE SAID. HE REPLIED, "IT IS NOT RIGHT TO TAKE THE CHILDREN'S BREAD AND TOSS IT TO THEIR DOGS." "YES, LORD," SHE SAID, "BUT EVEN THE DOGS EAT CRUMBS THAT FALL FROM THEIR MASTERS TABLE." THEN JESUS ANSWERED, "WOMAN, YOU HAVE GREAT FAITH! YOUR REQUEST IS GRANTED." AND HER DAUGHTER WAS HEALED AT THAT VERY HOUR.

So here we have a Canaanite woman, a foreigner, someone who was not part of the local church… I mean local synagogue; she didn't come from the same town, family or the same stream of ministry, and she is calling on the name of the Lord for mercy.

What do the Disciples of Christ do? They tell Jesus to send her away, because they considered her a pest, a nuisance. She was disrupting their groove, their worship time with Jesus. Her behavior is not in "ORDER" to their protocol.

Jesus remains quiet, which just increased this woman's tenacity; she gets more determined to seek Him out. This is where the woman's faith really plugs into God.

Jesus mentions to her that He was first sent to the Jews, yet she humbly replies that she was willing to take the remaining crumbs that were left over; this was because her faith was not shaken, she was not giving up, she was tenacious and pursued Him more.

This prompted Jesus to reply in this manner, "WOMAN, YOU HAVE GREAT FAITH. YOUR REQUEST IS GRANTED."

Jesus rebuked his disciples for not having faith throughout the Gospels, yet this outsider was bold enough to not care about what anyone thought about her or her actions; but pursued Jesus with all her might, and was said to have great faith. Amazing.

Today in the Church, we care excessively too much, about how we look or are represented to the public. The intended purpose of this is to make us look dignified and respectable; but it has come with a heavy cost us because it has compromised our faith.

We need to take a good look at ourselves both as an individual and as the Body of Christ, and deal with our unbelief. We need to get aggressive in our approach to God. We need to catch the fire, the passion to pursue Him at all costs. We need to be like the Canaanite woman by not caring what others think but only what God thinks.

Years ago after a late meeting in Tacoma, Washington; my team and I went to a Shari's Restaurant for a meal. There were some folks at the restaurant that recognized me from the revival meeting earlier that evening and so they asked me to lay hands on a friend of theirs who they had just led to the Lord. In other words, they wanted me to do this at the restaurant, right there, right now.

As I did, this young woman began to manifest a demonic spirit and she fell to the floor as the demon thrust her body around. I took authority over the demonic spirit and it left her.

As this was happening, the server walked through the doorway of the kitchen to our seating area and she saw this young woman being delivered from demons which might have seemed a bit intense with the young woman lying on the floor. The server was immediately freaked out; she tensed up, squealed, turned, and went back to the kitchen, never to return.

The atmosphere in that restaurant changed, and a number of people, maybe about 40 wanted me to pray for them. One by one, they were all overcome by the power of the Spirit and were laid out all over the floor. The presence of God was so thick in that place that anything could happen. One of the guys tried to get up off the floor and said: "I can't believe it, at Shari's Restaurant," only to be overcome by the Spirit a second time, and hit the ground.

Then I heard the voice of a man who was seated behind me eating his dinner with his wife. He told me that this was neither the time nor place, and that I should not have ministered to anyone there at all. For a moment, I thought about what he said, but then I realized what had just happened. God showed up at a restaurant! So I turned around and ignored him. I was not going to coddle his feelings, or be politically correct.

When God is into something, we should walk in that. We need to let go of the fear of man. Why should we care what others think? We shouldn't. We are on this Earth to please God, not man. If people get offended because you are walking in God's call for your life, too bad for them!

Each year we hold our annual Catch Heaven's Flame Conference. My friend David Hogan has been with us many times as a guest speaker. He has planted and is the overseer of over 1,000 churches and he ministers throughout the nations. David carries an aggressive faith stance and has seen healings of every kind, including 33 different people raised from the dead by his hands alone; and his ministry team has seen over 500 raised from the dead altogether.

One year, our largest financial contributor decided that if we wanted their churches continued financial support, they required of me to renounce my friendship with David and to renounce his ministry. I refused but thanked them for their previous support. Months later when we held our annual conference, David was scheduled to speak; I received disturbing and harassing emails from folks from that church because I didn't renounce David. Others gossiped and slandered me. I even lost friends from that local church because of this.

There comes a point where we have to draw the line and not care what others think. It frees us to pursue God. When we are not bound by the fear of MAN, we can genuinely chase God for supernatural miracles without hindrances that would otherwise hold us back.

Too much self-awareness can foster insecurities that are not healthy and do not come from God; and they are not full of faith either, but are rooted in fear.

For example, when Adam and Eve sinned, they immediately hid from God. The Canaanite woman's response was the exact opposite; she didn't hide, she was aggressive in her pursuit of Christ. She didn't care what was on the agenda, or that the disciples didn't want her around or even that her original cries seemed to be ignored by the Lord. She pursued Christ with her whole heart anyway. That should always be our response as well.

Chapter Nine

The Relationship of Hope & Faith

Many people today get hope and faith confused. Hope is an expectation. Faith is the link between you and God regarding that expectation.

God given expectations are by nature full peace and joy. This is why hope is so important. Hope is the expectation of a promise from God. It holds within itself trust in Him.

Faith however, is the actual title deed of something He has promised (*given*) to us. In other words, we own it; it has become part of our inheritance.

Hebrews 11:1 says: "NOW FAITH IS THE SUBSTANCE OF THINGS HOPED FOR, THE EVIDENCE OF THINGS NOT SEEN."

The Word of God gives hope. When the Spirit breaths on a specific portion of Scripture, He brings revelation to a specific matter, thus, God highlights this specific matter so that faith can then arise on that verse. Remember that faith comes by hearing, and hearing by a Word from God.

Therefore, the relationship between hope and faith are closely related because they work together. We can't have faith without hope. Faith follows hope in sequence.

Hope anticipates, typically with some measure of pleasure and confidence because it is full of joy and peace as it trusts in God. Faith feeds hope with specifics by turning hope (*expectation*) into an actual promise. Hope is a gift from God; it is part of our inheritance.

Romans 5:5 says: "AND HOPE DOES NOT DISAPPOINT US, BECAUSE GOD HAS POURED OUT HIS LOVE INTO OUR HEARTS, BY THE HOLY SPIRIT, WHOM HE HAS GIVEN US."

Demons understand this and try to steal away our hope, knowing that by doing so; they can undercut the promises of God and kill our faith. The loss of hope (*expectation*) can abort the fulfillment of God's promise.

Proverbs 13:12 says:

"HOPE DIFFERED MAKES THE HEART SICK..."

If the enemy can steal away our hope and get us to doubt God, then the faith connection to our promise will break, bringing a disconnection; thus preventing us from taking hold of what God has promised.

Sometimes God reveals the end (*our promise*) from the beginning. This is to give us hope (*expectation*), so that as we journey through the process, we will indeed one day take hold of our inheritance; (*God's promise*). Then as we go through the process, we can link with God (*connecting by faith*), to bring about the fulfilment of hope (expectation).

Now it is important that connecting by faith might require actual steps to be taken in order to align with hope (*expectation*). Remember, faith without works is dead (James 2). So we **must** apply our works (*deeds*) in alignment to our hope (*expectation*) by faith.

God has given my wife and I, a lot of promises which we know are ours. However, through the years we went through many testing's, trials and tribulations and have had to pay a heavy price to see them come to pass.

During these trials and tribulations, we were not only tested with our faith but the enemy tried to take away our hope. We went through a time when everything fell apart. It was during that season of my life that I realized the value and relationship of hope in how it pertains to the working of faith.

Romans 15:13 says:

"MAY THE GOD OF HOPE FILL YOU WITH ALL JOY AND PEACE AS YOU TRUST IN HIM, SO THAT YOU MAY OVERFLOW WITH HOPE BY THE POWER OF THE HOLY SPIRIT."

As I have mentioned here, hope is an expectation of a promise. Therefore we can cultivate our faith by first: Keeping hope, that God given expectation (promise), right in front of us. In other words, put it at the center of your attention. Cultivate what God wants to create.

Here is a practical tool that will help with this:

First, take a moment to visualize a clear-cut picture of something God has promised you, and then meditate on God's written Word (*Scriptures that relate to that promise*) and what He has said to you concerning that promise.

Second: Continue to exercise faith by demonstrating God's Word, even if you don't see immediate results. This is where we begin to walk by faith and not by sight! Maybe the circumstances fly in the face of God's written Word and what He has spoken to you; that however, doesn't matter. What you sow is what you will reap, therefore speak, declare and walk on God's Word, live it out.

As you do this, proceed to write down everything the Lord speaks to you about your promise, and then pray over what He tells you, so that you will be able to call those things which are not, as they are (Romans 4:17). By doing this, you will put into your heart the assurance of the answer.

Hope is a good thing, in fact it is a God thing; we all have need of hope. As long as we have hope, we can cope with anything this world or the Devil sends our way.

Just because we don't experience immediate breakthrough, doesn't mean that the promises of God will not come to pass. God's Word is true. Sometimes we have to keep on hoping even though it looks as if all hope is dead. This was certainly the case with Abraham as he and Sarah were awaiting the birth of their promised son, Isaac:

Romans 4:18 says:

"IN HOPE AGAINST HOPE HE BELIEVED, IN ORDER THAT HE MIGHT BECOME THE FATHER OF MANY NATIONS, ACCORDING TO THAT WHICH HAD BEEN SPOKEN, "SO SHALL YOUR DECEDENTS BE."

If Abraham's faith had been based solely upon his circumstances, his hope probably would have been shattered. However, Abraham's hope was in God, and he received his hope (*promise*)!

Remember that God rewards the passionate heart, not the casual inquire. You cannot be laid back and nonchalant in your requests and expect to get answers. Hearts full of red-hot desire gets result.

Psalm 37:4 says:

"DELIGHT YOURSELF IN THE LORD; AND HE WILL GIVE YOU THE DESIRES OF YOUR HEART."

Chapter Ten

The Power of Words

Have you ever considered how much power there is in what we say? Though it may not be visible to the naked eye, there are both positive and negative forces that are put to work when we speak.

Luke 6:45 says:

A GOOD MAN BRINGS GOOD THINGS OUT OF THE GOOD STORED UP IN HIS HEART, AND AN EVIL MAN BRINGS EVIL THINGS OUT OF THE EVIL STORED UP IN HIS HEART. FOR THE OUT OF THE OVERFLOW OF HIS HEART, HIS MOUTH SPEAKS.

When we speak, something deep inside of us is released and things get set in motion; a cause and effect takes place. Words can be used to build up or to tear down, to cause life or bring death; to release faith or even unbelief.

Remember, Jesus Himself cursed a tree with His words and it withered all the way to the roots! Jesus went on to explain that if we have faith in our heart and speak to a mountain, it will move. Therefore our words are very powerful.

Proverbs 18:21says:

"LIFE AND DEATH ARE IN THE POWER OF THE TONGUE..."

Psalm 33:6 says:

"BY THE **WORD** OF THE LORD THE HEAVENS WERE MADE ..." Verse 9 continues: "FOR HE **SPOKE**, AND IT CAME TO BE; HE **COMMANDED**, AND IT STOOD FIRM..."

The book of beginnings (Genesis) reveals that God spoke the universe into being. In fact, God released His faith through the creative power of His spoken word. Think about that for a minute; God's power is so awesome that all He had to do was speak and matter was created out of nothing. God said, "LET THERE BE LIGHT; AND THERE WAS LIGHT" (Genesis 1:3).

The universe and everything in it was created by God's spoken Word; even today all things are sustained by that same power. Remember, Jesus is the Word; and we need His Word to be alive and flowing through our being and out from our mouths.

Through the Word we can do the impossible; and by His Word the impossible becomes possible. This is also why reading, meditating and confessing the Word is so important.

John 6:63 says:

THE WORDS I HAVE SPOKEN TO YOU ARE SPIRIT AND THEY ARE LIFE.

Therefore our tongue is a powerful tool when yielded to the Lord. However, it is important to guard our words, because what we sow we reap; and if we are speaking negative words concerning our situation, we can unduly set the wrong things into motion.

Negative words can damage your physical body, corrupt your thought life, destroy your emotions, bring harm to those around you, which can bring about lasting devastation to your circumstances and ultimately bring you to ruin.

Proverbs 12:18 says:

RECKLESS WORDS PIERCE LIKE A SWORD, BUT THE TONGUE OF THE WISE BRINGS HEALING.

Demons can use your own negative words against you to crush you; however your words can also defeat them! Revelation 12:11 says: "THEY OVERCAME THE DEVIL, BY THE BLOOD OF THE LAMB, BY THE **WORD** OF THEIR TESTIMONY..." Remember, we can overcome demons by our words!

[3]Few, if any of us, get through life without having negative words spoken against us. Gossip, slander, false accusations, lies, the list goes on. If something negative has been said about you, or if you have been falsely accused, don't try to fight it in a natural way. Condemn the words spoken against you in the name of Jesus in private. Never condemn the individual, only their words. Then claim what God has given to you by faith.

---

[3] Mega Faith – by Marilyn Hickey

Isaiah 54:17 says:

"NO WEAPON FORMED AGAINST YOU SHALL PROSPER; AND EVERY TONGUE WHICH RISES UP AGAINST YOU SHALL BE CONDEMNED. THIS IS THE HERITAGE OF THE SERVANTS OF THE LORD, AND THIS IS THE VINDICATION FROM ME," DECLARES THE LORD.

In today's culture, humor plays a significant role in our daily lives. Unfortunatly, much of it is perverse and actually has a destructive element to it. When this is the case, it is not faith building but actually gives birth to unbelief.

Ephesians 5:4 says:

NOR SHOULD THERE BE OBSCENITY, FOOLISH TALK OR COARSE JOKING, WHICH ARE OUT OF PLACE, BUT RATHER THANKSGIVING.

As believers, we are not to be guided by our culture, which getting more corrupt by the minute, but guided by God's Word, which never changes. We should fix our minds on things above and not on things below.

Growing up as a young man, my dad always repeated an old saying: "Loose lips sink ships." In World War Two, it was used as a warning to sailors. If those on the radio said too much, it could give away the Allies ship locations; and the Nazi submarines would then sink them. In a similar way, if we are not guarding our words, we will say too much until we end up saying the wrongs things.

Proverbs 21:23 says:

HE WHO GUARDS HIS MOUTH AND HIS TONGUE KEEPS HIMSELF FROM CALAMITY.

My father was trying to give me a solid piece of advice. We need to choose our words carefully and not talk just for the sake of talking. There is no good in that. We need to be specific with our words or not say anything at all.

My Grandfather, through his lifestyle, had another powerful lesson that shaped my life. Every time he got out of a chair or went into another room he said: "*Praise the Lord*." Literally forty to fifty times a day, anytime he was transitioning from one thing to another he said: "*Praise the Lord.*"

Praise plays a key role in faith. Psalm 150 tells us again and again to praise the Lord for His mighty works and to magnify His Name: "LET EVERYTHING THAT HAS BREATH PRAISE THE LORD."

Psalm 100:4 says:

ENTER HIS GATES WITH THANKSGIVING AND HIS COURTS WITH PRAISE; GIVE THANKS TO HIM AND PRAISE HIS NAME.

In 2007 I started working with Evangelist Hamilton Filmalter. Now Hamilton has this thing about giving glory to Jesus. There have been many occasions he and I have walked into various venues, including Starbucks, when suddenly Hamilton announces with a loud voice: "*Thank You Jesus.*" After ministering alongside of Hamilton for years now, I picked it up. Now I say "*Thank You Jesus*" all of the time. Let me tell you, when you say: "Thank you Jesus" over and over; in public and private settings, it increases your faith.

An attitude of praise is a great witness to unbelievers. The world is harsh. People are used to hearing all the gossip, slander and backbiting. Yet, when a believer is full of praise even in the mist of difficulty, it communicates real faith. Unbelievers won't initially understand it, but it can give them hope. This is alone is a good reason to watch the words we speak.

Each and every day, we should give thanks and praise God. Psalms 118:24 says: "THIS IS THE DAY WHICH THE LORD HAS MADE; LET US REJOICE AND BE GLAD IN IT". I want to encourage you to look at this way: Faith is like a muscle; in order for it to grow, we must exercise it. Praise is one of the best ways to build our faith up. When we do, it is like a sunrise; it's fresh every morning.

Chapter Eleven

Faith Builders

Romans says faith comes from hearing and hearing by the Word of God. Therefore, I have prepared faith building confessions that I have derived from the Bible that will strengthen your faith.

Take a few minutes to read these Bible confessions **OUT LOUD**. Confess, declare, prophesy and speak God's Word over your life. Meditate on their meaning and allow it to get into your spirit.

There is actual scientific evidence that when you read out loud, the neurons in the brain are stimulated and become active in a way that is never achieved just by reading silently, in your mind to yourself. This is why God instructed the Israelites to read and sing scripture out loud in ancient times; and how they could memorize entire books of the Old Testament.

There is something powerful about confessing God's Word. As you do this, do not stop there. The enemy on your shoulder will try to convince you that you did enough. No. Do it again and again. Keep on contending. Keep on pressing and claiming these confessions as your own. Take ownership of them. As you do, they will take a life on their own.

I pray that out of His glorious riches, that Christ may be strengthened in me with the power of the Spirit in my inner being, so that Christ may dwell in my heart through faith. **Ephesians 3:16-17**

The just shall live by faith. **Romans 1:17**

Without faith it is impossible to please God. **Hebrews 11:6**

Everything that does not come from faith is sin. **Romans 14:23**

Faith comes by hearing, and hearing by the Word of God. **Romans 10:17**

Now faith is the substance of things hoped for, the evidence (the title deed) of things not seen. **Hebrews 11:1**

I walk by faith and not by sight. **2 Corinthians 5:7**

I have been given the ability of faith by the Spirit of God. **1 Corinthians 12:9**

I overcome the enemy, because greater is Christ in me, than demons in the world. **1 John 4:4**

What shall we then say to these things? If God be for us, who can be against us? **Romans 8:31**

Out of the abundance of the heart the mouth speaks, therefore I speak words of faith. **Matthew 12:34**

Life and death are in the power of the tongue, therefore by faith I speak life. **Proverbs 18:21**

By faith in God, ALL things are possible. **Mark 10:27**

Jesus said: Anyone who has faith in Me, will do greater things than these. **John 14:12**

My actions shall demonstrate faith, and I have faith, a faith that is alive and active in deeds. **James 2:18-24**

I am full of faith and in the Holy Spirit. **Acts 6:5**

By faith I stand firm. **2 Corinthians 1:24**

I am standing firm in the faith. **1 Corinthians 16:13**

I am filled with joy because I believe. **Acts 16:34**

Jesus is the author and finisher of my faith. **Hebrews 12:2**

I am happy in my faith; I rejoice and will be happy in my heart. **1 Thessalonians 5:16**

Because I am a believer, I am now happy glad, full of joy and I shall rejoice before God. **Psalm 68:3**

Everything is possible for him who believes. **Mark 9:23**

According to my faith it will be done. **Matthew 9:29**

With God All things are possible. **Matthew 19:26**

By even the smallest of faith, even that of a mustard seed; I can say to this mountain: "Move from here to there" and it will be moved. **Matthew 17:20**

I already know how to give good gifts to my children, how much more the Father in heaven, give the Spirit when I ask Him. **Luke 11:13**

By faith I understand that the worlds were prepared by the Word of God, so that what is seen was not made out of things which are visible. **Hebrews 11:3**

These three remain: Faith, hope and love and the greatest of these is love. **Ephesians 5:25**

References

Chapter One

1. Bonnke, Reinhard. Faith – The Link with God's Power: 2003

Chapter Three

2. Bonnke, Reinhard. Faith – The Link with God's Power: 2003

3. Hickey, Marilyn. Mega Faith: 2001

SD - #0053 - 060826 - C0 - 229/152/6 - PB - 9781312027213 - Gloss Lamination